THIS IS
THE STORY
OF HIS LIFE

THIS IS THE STORY OF HIS LIFE

TJ BEITELMAN

Black
Lawrence
Press

Black
Lawrence
Press

www.blacklawrence.com

Executive Editor: Diane Goettel
Book and Cover Design: Amy Freels

Copyright © 2018 TJ Beitelman
ISBN: 978-1-62557-985-0

Published 2018 by Black Lawrence Press.
Printed in the United States.

—CONTENTS—

Endings

—BEGINNINGS—

———

The Dream of Flight

This is the story of his life he drew up around himself: is what he
was trapped or *wombed*? Midair? In a clot of migratory birds?

———so loud were the beating wings. Some nearby land
mass, sheer audacious face or iconic ridge of ice or else
rock or even some larger Something-Else than just this
collective self for the sound to bounce off or crash into...

He was trapped. Or wombed. *Midair.*

...not like cymbals.
A very thudding sound like heavy hooves on soft earth.
Mud in my mouth a quarter-mile up. One of us fell
tumbling wing-over-wing. One and one and one more
again. Others of us veered lightward. Any common star
is also a singular sun. Any distance is a distance you can
fly to. If that is a sun waits at the end of it...

Once he found himself entombed in a singular body of birds.

...which is not true because things die: they
crash or turn away. Tumble down...

Not many sets of wings but just one single set of wings.

A single-minded purpose of here-to-there. Mad-winged exertion. Thud and thud and thud again. Breast plate dappled with mud.

The thing he was in was in the air.

It was headed somewhere.

... there are too far distances ...

Somewhere was a faraway place he had been to before.

The whole thing had always had wings.

The whole thing had always been alive

en route

... flying is an impossible thing for almost every wingless thing conceived.——

and it always would be.

————

Noah

This is the story of his life he drew up around himself: that it could
fit inside a box

————*2-X-2.*————

Mama Giraffe and Papa Giraffe and the entire City of Mice
because they are all each so tiny.

This explains how he now scurries and his long neck. His taste for
tucked away little holes and the tenderest leaves atop the tall trees.

Or else the 2 is a short distance

                                                    and the 2 is a short distance

and so: he must write so-small in his so-cramped hand as to not
even bother to put it all down in words——————

―――――

The Toy Boat

This is the story of his life he drew up around himself: when he was a boy he sent in the one toy boat he had made with his own bare hands to the Toy Boat You Have Made With Your Own Bare Hands Contest.

Except it was not a toy boat but the story of a toy boat.

Except it was not the story of a toy boat but a poem.

Except it was not a poem but notes for a poem.

Except it was not notes for a poem but his math homework.

Fractions.

One-fourth plus three-sevenths. Seven-tenths minus a third.

None of the answers were answers that he knew. He put his name and left all the other blanks blank.

He won. All the other toy boats sank.

———

Event Horizon: Original Sin

This is the story of his life he drew up around himself: it was invariable then that he would know just enough to get himself hanged.

———*Do you have any dietary restrictions*———

He knew enough to ask her this.

But not enough to know that St. Augustine was off limits. Entirely. Be it town or theologian.

She turned against him then and there forevermore.

And anyway it was not Augustine in his mind but the madman with the sermons for birds because early on she had indicated her especial affinity for wings.

She said for instance she could abide the idea of cherubs.

Later it turned out he knew nothing which it turned out was much safer.

Angel is what they called their only child.

Monkey Mind

This is the story of his life he drew up around himself: the problem of sleep and days-on-end with none of it to speak of.

A consistent ache in the small of his back.

The clocks slow ticking. Or noiseless light of what were not ticks anymore but an incessant mechanized mind keeping track. One through sixty a second nature. Counting piled on top of counting.

> ——*I go backwards from some large number. Or else an alphabet. Lose track. Start again. Go again. Again. Again. What is the trick involving sheep. Warm milk. The cow jumps over the moon. Forget fish: do monkeys ever sleep. We monkeys descended from monkeys descended from trees. Hands for feet. Long tail another kind of limb. Swing. Reach. Search. The ground a foreign surface teeming with living dangers. Head on a swivel. Mind inside that won't shut off.*——

He is this little monkey in a box. It is very dark.

He's counting down the days.

─────

Event Horizon: Metastasis

This is the story of his life he drew up around himself: the beloved pet dog has a hole in her ear or else the hole in her ear is what he imagines will be born when they pluck the black growth from inside it.

Or else she herself will dig it out on accident with her delicate hind-leg scratching.

Which is exactly what happens.

The growth is tender as new growth.

The tender green shoot reaches. A newborn's fingernail is parchment-thin. For a certain time what bleeds

                                              is always still

alive.

―――

The Talk

This is the story of his life he drew up around himself: Angel said
Father I've married the Falconer and he was taken aback.

Your mother loved wings is what he thought and so it was what he
thought to say:

―――*Your mother loved wings.*―――

I'll be relocating she said. A faraway look in her eye. As far away
I'm afraid as a ~~gyre~~ girl can go. She cried. She said it's not because
I want to it's because I have to. I love the Falconer. He lives by the
sea. He says he's been left before.

―――*the sea? The sea! St. Francis of Assisi! That's his*
name...―――

Is what he said.

None of which is true but he said it over and over again.

As if it could replace all the things he hadn't known

and all the things too he had forgot

at first or ever lost.

———

Event Horizon: MRI

This is the story of his life he drew up around himself: they take a shady picture of his brain and ferret out an incidental hole.

———*right frontal lobe.*———

It is then and only then that words become somewhat more strange.

Hole and lobe and lope and mole.

Elope which he had done.

The peace or the piece of the Justice.

———*I do I've done I'm done.*———

A ring is a kind of hole.

His finger is no ferret but a shy rabbit without warren or incident. Looking to disappear.

The Talk with Talk of Being Rent in Two

This is the story of his life he drew up around himself: Angel said
Father I've married the Wolfman and this time he knew what to
expect.

She would tear up

———*tear or tear.*———

and say she must go far away. Not because she
wants to but because she has to. Love was a nothing he knew now
turned out safer.

Which is not true.

———*your mother . . .*

is what he said instead

. . . loved all animals equal.———

———

Event Horizon: Oedipus

This is the story of his life he drew up around himself: he fancied himself a young man who was not a young man at all but one who was already old or at least a young man who had been aspiring to advanced years all his life.

> ———*a parable: in another world, an Old Man carries*
> *the book of your life in his pocket much as one might*
> *carry a cherished book of poems. There are dog ears.*
> *Smudges of grease where he got his lunch on it. Three*
> *pages he rips out and tapes them to his bedroom wall.*
> *Because he loves them so . . . ———*

He thought of himself as a young man who was not a young man at all but one whose life was already missing three pages.

An old man is a man who rips the middles out of things even or especially if he loves them.

Polonius

This is the story of his life he drew up around himself: the capsule of a portentous dream.

> ——*I was chosen for the part of the boy whose loves are over and over again unrequited. I knew it was a part I could play. I wanted that stage. I wanted my lines. I wasn't the lead but that wasn't what I wanted at all. I wanted to steal scene after scene. More tortured prince than the tortured prince. Mad display to put the world on notice.——*

The talking cure is dead. To cure is not to treat.

A dream is up for grabs. Anyone's guess. One stabs a snake with his mother's favorite carving knife. In her bed. This means the intellectual stores of civilization and specifically free-market capitalism won't fit anymore in any brain-sized thing.

Or something.

Or else we push our bodies out into the light of the waking world in order to escape an intricate system of unreliable gods and monsters girding up a vaster darker world behind our eyes.

——but then I discovered it wasn't as I thought at all.
O no! I was to be the old man mired in protocols and
paradox. Fit to start a scene or two. Etc. The unlucky one
mistaken for the villain shrouded behind a curtain in
the mad prince's mum's bedchamber. Stabbed through
unseen on a hunch. Or a whim. Or both. Almost just an
afterthought.——

To sleep perchance to dream.

The butterfly dreams Zhuangzi. Yon cloud shaped like a camel a
weasel a dagger a dream. A butterfly.

Whatever else the mad prince has him say it is.

The Dream of Beginnings and Endings

This is the story of his life he drew up around himself: *every happy family.* Etc.

An unhappy family. Etc.

His Tolstoy forms a dumbshow. Clowns and greasepaint.

Clowns have their particular greasepaint smell and this he carries with him for the rest of his natural born days. The sword swallower was a mensch.

Etc.

> ——*it was the best of times. It was the worst of times.*——

That one he read as a boy in the smart class at school. All of them piled in one of those tiny cars and zoomed off down the Ninth Grade Hallway. Helter-skelter madcap swerves. They tumbled out on top of each other at the threshold of Mrs. Borden's

> ——*not her name. Or was it.*——

classroom. Big shoes orange hair. Squeaks
honks a rimshot.

A far far better thing. Then the punchline guillotine.

Multiple Choice

This is the story of his life he drew up around himself: there was the precise moment when he said to himself almost out loud

——*none of us will ever be more beautiful than we are right now.*——

He was still a boy almost. He sat in something like an auditorium. Rows and rows of hard-backed green seats. Cinderblock walls and linoleum floors. A schooling milieu. Him one of dozens of adolescents submerged in a tank of silence save for the odd intermittent sigh or dropped No. 2 pencil. The interminable turning of test booklets one thin page at a time. The standardized cadence of what they all were together.

——*I'm not saying we're all each beautiful or that I am or you are. I'm not even saying that as one Collective Thing we are a beautiful collective thing. I'm saying we've all each reached our high-water mark. What I'm saying is it's all downhill from here.*——

Two trains leave the station. Different times.

Or else the same time.

Either way they travel at different rates of speed. Down different tracks.

There are other accountable variables as well: piles of coal of variant sizes shoveled with more or less dispatch into more or less hot furnaces. The respective weights of the dining cars. If there is a jazz band on board. Uphill. Downhill. Against the wind. With it.

Anyway. Solve for each of the following: the precise moment to six decimals the world ends. The fate of human intimacy and network TV. Will there still be books.

True or False: there will be flying cars in our lifetime.

Define our lifetime.

The likelihood of life on other planets.

If you had to choose between which of your future children would lose an eye or an arm or both which would you choose and why.

If you had to choose between which of your parents outlives you which would you choose and why.

If you had to choose between knowing everything or knowing nothing or knowing only what you could do nothing about which and why in that case too.

Rest easy. What you've heard is true.

We are of course supposed to guess.

———

The Talk with Talk of Sport

This is the story of his life he drew up around himself: Angel said Father I've married the King of the Hardwood and he is so often out of breath and I breathe into him. His long bones ache. All morning is us lacing his sneakers. It is more than I believe I can do to make him whole.

There is just so much of him.

He spreads his arms wide.

> ———*our arms are not our arms but wings. Our bones*
> *not bones but words for bones. Our words are not words*
> *but prayers. Five. Four. Three. Two. One.*———

He puts up a prayer and it dances

on the breakaway rim.

―――

Muse

This is the story of his life he drew up around himself: she stopped midstream.

A sentence is a stream.

A froth of swift-moving ~~sentiment~~—sediment. What unseen creatures thrive there or do not.

He stamped across yon field into a hilly green ~~word~~—wood. To hide.

Hiding is a thing human beings do. All animals do it.

He stepped into the cold stream and up was a whole alley of things leading to the free blue sky.

> ――*pretend you know I'm here. Pretend you know I*
> *need you to read my mind. Pretend echolocation at*
> *least. I came so far and have come so close—close the*
> *distance between this and that half of my half-hearted—*
> *heart… yes: heart―――*

Her mind was a stream. Lord and it was so swift so dark. Beautiful and cold. The body of her words her world. The body of her body.

——*body is a word for beauty.*——

And so he had no choice but to believe it all was real.

Hairshirt

This is the story of his life he drew up around himself: a collection of personal miscellany and minutiae.

All the words that had failed him.

Where scars used to be. If it rained on his birthday or a cold Lord's day in June. How much string and spit and gum is useful in a lifetime. Every sales receipt a villanelle a sestina a road map. His time-stamped time. His accounting.

The accounting of his accounting.

There is nothing he can say he fashioned with his hands.

> ———*I gave up*
> *trying to put the world in my mouth one piece at a time.*
> *Only saints should be so patient or so empty.*———

———

Birth

This is the story of his life he drew up around himself: this Muse's face is not a face instead it is a sage's wizened visage.

The Old Woman wears the echo of her pretty young face.

The world she's made is a warm wet place.

More warm and wet than what we ever needed it to be. *Wanting* is another thing.

　　——for instance bite what swells to keep it swelling is a
　　trick I am learning to do.——

What he makes makes homage to the world

　　——warm. Wet.——

　　　　　　　　　　　　　　　　　　　she's slit him
from throat to groin.

―――――

Event Horizon: Surface Tension

This is the story of his life he drew up around himself:

―――*I felt water before wet. Skin-on-skin.*―――

Here is what happened.

He brought his hand near nearer nearest to the surface of a pool of warm water.

Or he did no bringing at all.

His hand brought itself.

The surface brought itself.

His mind attended after the fact. Minds do this.

My skin is wet is what he thought after it happened except the trick was it hadn't happened yet.

Something in his hand or the water or another something altogether stopped.

One touched the other and-but-or there was no record of the touching.

There is no word for the way his hand was not wet. *Dry* contains no *should have been.*

—*I think things with skins are everywhere. Permeable another word for something I do not want inside me is inside me.*—

The pen falls in and breaks the skin.

—*skin then is the word for please god cut me open.*—

―――――

The Talk with Talk of Something Cosmic

This is the story of his life he drew up around himself: Angel said
Father I've married the man who each morning dims the stars of
the sky. The mechanics are a puzzle. Surely it helps his arms are so
long. That part I can suss.

But it's just so much for a single man to do.

　　　―――he flies.―――

The stars are numberless limitless she said.

　　　―――it's a chain reaction. Like dominoes. The
　　　Universe.―――

But it happens in a blink she said. He tells me it's a simple trick of
peripheries.

What you look straight at is never what you think you see.

There's a whole mess of worlds the light of day obscures.

I've gotten myself mixed up with an illusionist. But he doesn't
miss a day. Constancy counts for something.

Also all the worlds in me a man like him can reach to.

Rebirth

This is the story of his life he drew up around himself: a vow to use his powers only for the greater good. Easter Day is the day of one particularly prominent version of the Risen Lord. Something in particular re: crowing cocks denial.

The Superpower of Grace. Humility. Humiliation.

Sucking vinegar off the sponge.

Also the ascetic Superpower of crucifixion which is to say some manner of spike spiked through the web of bones scaffolding a palm a palm and two stacked ankles.

And then we put this high up on display. For all of us to see.

Also the Superpower of all those pretty Marys come to dig him from the tomb.

——mine is a paltry power and too easy to mis-
appropriate. The power to traipse between worlds but
not the power to tell which one is real.——

An Easter Day in the modern age. A plastic steakhouse peopled half-full of half-drunk shades. Well-muscled men tattooed in sadness gulp bad beer and suck dry the bones of chicken wings.

They pass a smart-phone with messy hands. They say into it baby doll. To whom this disembodied baby doll belongs

      ——*I belong to the Whole Universe the Whole Sky. I gave my only begotten Son which is an All-Inclusive EZPass to pass unseen to pass thru walls to see you when you're sleeping to know when you're awake which is not true which would be weird which would not even at all be appropriate and which is also technically impossible for a corporeal body and maybe even blasphemy two times over——*

      no one can be for sure. This is the provinces. Long ago some surely saner man washed his hands of all it. Surely.

The pink red meat he eats came from far away on a truck driven by some surely sleepy man.

The piped-in sound is the sound of the buzzing refrigerator but someone somewhere wrote it down: *your skin as sweet as moonlight / touch is like the sugar baby baby baby doll.*

Or something.

There are hostesses possessed of fine bone structure. This is the custom. These are girls. These are babies. Dolled up.

The other man with the ornate armless shirt gave the one called Laci twenty dollars just to open the door. A dollar per year on God's green earth then tip her tip at 25%. Which is the cryptic calculus of just how young she really is.

Which is to say sixteen.

She has come to dig him into the tomb spiked through a web of bones silkscreened onto his shirt.

This is Easter Day for God's sake.

>—now now. These are the provinces but there's surely
>no one left to wash his hands of us. Not now.——

'In your heart of hearts' the one says to the other and so then getting at the very heart of things must be his Superpower and there is the chance then he too has vowed to only use his powers to advance the greater good.

Which is not true.

This man's Superpower is handing out Andrew Jacksons to pretty adolescent girls.

His Superpower is stealing back into the tomb.

Tomb could almost be

>——(write it!) Womb.——

> more than almost its opposite.

The opposite of risen is fallen.

The image of the fallen basketball star flashes on all the screens mounted up above us.

For all to see.

He wears an Endtimes beard. Locusts. Honey. Lay-ups.

Once he brought real guns to the arena. Once he shat in a teammate's shoe. He has always been a problem.

But once upon a time he could shoot. Anywhere. Anytime.

Let us play the game then where we see how many silent TV screens we can all ignore. If the volume's off and no one watches does the crucified Endtimes-gunner still lead the team in shots?

This is the story of faith in just outcomes.

This is story of his life.

He said he would only use his powers for good but then that was fine because then he had powers.

His was the Superpower to be seen and not heard.

Which was the Superpower of the children of yesteryear. When the plastic world was really very real.

———*I like Ike!*———

Etc.

The Fallen Hoopster rises in the lane to loft an ill-advised running one-hander. The ball sticks in the well of his palm and is summarily slapped away.

His is now a different power. The power to be a shadow of what you used to be.

The Superpower of what are called ghosts.

This is not a power per se.

This is just a problem.

Forever and always it has come to no good end.

—MIDDLES—

Moving Pictures

This is the story of his life he drew up around himself: in the modern age the business of making what is not real real involves attachments.

Attaching things to other things.

Affix small pieces of light to a system of spots on a pixelated body in motion.

> ——*an uninterrupted body in motion tends to stay in*
> *motion. Bodies at rest stay resting. This is what is called*
> *inertia and there must be a reason for it.——*

The body is not a system. Track the body of lights using a system of intricate machines.

The body is not a machine. It's built of a system of breakable bones. Bones attached to other bones.

The magic of industry is the industry of light.

Industrial Magic. And Light.

Intricate. Etc.

The machine churns out an imaginary man. In motion. Whole cities of them. If you can make a city you can make a world. Worlds and cities full of bones inside of bodies and also light but no physics.

Or new physics. Selective and capricious.

Or insouciant.

A sad-old-man's house lifts off under the power of many hundreds of thousands of helium-filled balloons. You are to believe the lonely man attached them by his lonesome one by one.

Talking dogs fall from great heights and they live. They *talk*. Almost nothing ever dies.

> ——*it's not the same. I'm serious. I'm serious. Listen. They did that just to make you think you could.*——

Still Life with Fred Rogers

This is the story of his life he drew up around himself: he took a
guilty pleasure in putting it all down in parts. Line shape color
texture value in no particular order.

Drips and smudges.

The paint on his pants his hands his shoes. Primal spatter-figures
ambulate in the background.

Make no mistake.

Composition is a mess.

He makes a collage of bailbonds bumper stickers shopping bags
with handles *NYT* obits. Pollock put on different shoes

⸻*so too Fred Rogers. Would you could you won't you
be my…*⸻

to steal us to his land of make-believe.

———————

Still Life with Suburbs, Part I

This is the story of his life he drew up around himself:

———*you would you could you won't.*———

Which is to say the story of his life was a gray and windy day.

Some anonymous American city of middle-size and middle-distance. Breeze-bent trees yearn in one direction.

Her want her wont her won't.

Drag the recycling to the curb.

———*"if the world was not round…"*———

Etc.

———*"…you would not be on top of me"*———

Etc.

The neighbor prunes the azalea down to nothing but a bonsai and an adjacent pile of living bones.

Only A-to-B but such altogether different things.

                                       Ding-ding
comes the trolley to take it all away.

Still Life with Suburbs, Part II

This is the story of his life he drew up around himself: he traveled down a cul de sac and now he trudges back.

The days on end are no atomized living series.

The night is very dark and too warm for this jacket so he drags it behind him. Some dog is trapped in some somewhere domestication. A tall wire fence around a yard.

House after house just like the days on end are no atomized living etc.

Draw yourself inside a real thing.

Even a flat-planed box on paper is real. You are the man made of simple sticks.

——*sticks and stones may break my bones. Etc.*——

Bones are sticks and break themselves. It's true.

Words are something else but they too break things and you break them.

By you I mean him or even me which simply could not be a bigger problem. It comes to no good end.

But back to trudging back. The dog's voice calls from the other side of somewhere. Somewhere warm and wet. No: dark and warm. The dog's voice calls and calls and then it stops. He lets the jacket drop.

Still Life with Jihad

This is the story of his life he drew up around himself: dateline: an Abbottabad of his own conception.

Which is to say nine years slow and plain. Hiding out. A valley. Green hills all around.

And a fortress of walls inside of walls inside of walls he has erected. Not one but two security gates. A dusty square dungeon.

There he jails with him anyone he is rumored to have loved.

Once to go from one room or cell in his mind to another room or cell in his mind he took up a heavy sledgehammer in his mind's own bare hands. With that he bludgeoned out a man-sized hole in the one sturdy wall between them. A hole rough and unfinished but it did what all holes do.

> ——*As do commandos. Commandos find the guy who leads to the guy who leads to the guy who leads to the guy. The guy holed up. Or else it is the opposite but in the end they find the guy just the same.——*

He is the guy. In there. Somewhere.

Behind the walls and the walls and the wives.

Your commando mission is this: Find. Fix. Finish.

The guerilla warrior. His one-man holy war.

You will encounter blowback. Etc. A firefight for sure. Human shields. This is not some craggy mountain. This is not some dripping cave. This is his sleepy million-dollar getaway.

Plant a pair of bullets in his eye. Two rough holes to find and fix and finish him.

Scuttle your collaterally failed flying machine. Abscond with his body in the extra helicopter you've been clever enough to think to bring.

Swab his cheek. For cells. Take pictures. For proof.

Show no one.

Anoint the corpse. Wrap it face it east and bag it in a heavy bag. Work fast. The world waits. Awaits.

Lay this dead thing once and for all on a flat board. Slide it still and quiet into the choppy indeterminate sea. No. There is no other place for it—

—*and now you can*
never do another thing wrong.——

Still Life with Sirens

This is the story of his life he drew up around himself: the sirens sounded for a time and then they stopped. What you did then was up to you.

He always took this as a given.

The squall line was the variable.

Would it ever find him and when it did where on God's green earth would it sweep him to?

Once he swept himself all the way to the American cradle of New England. To be lost. And found.

Or it was not once but so many times he could not count them on all his fingers and toes. More times than he has bones in his body plus teeth in his head.

Which is not true. It was approximately seven, give or take.

He was never found but soon that became not the point at all. The point was the call and what called him. Then the point of no return.

Seven give-or-take times he took the time to tie himself to the mast. Just in case. The sirens sounded for a time and then they stopped. Sounded.

——what sweet birds chatter at the call of an ill-defined
coming catastrophe.——

Stopped.

In an upstairs room he sensed the black-eyed poet's-poet's shade in scrimmy white. She was there somewhere.

All he had to do was look. He shut his eyes tight.

Made with his own bare hands a simple cabin in the woods of his own mind. Planted rows of beans for sustenance. And sat.

It was not a real ship. There was no mast.

The sirens called and called and then they stopped.

He lived deliberately and upon deliberation found he had not lived at all.

Still Life with Philippe Petit

This is the story of his life he drew up around himself:

> ——*love or thwarted love is the root of all I do. How*
> *could I deny it.*——

Which is to say this is not a story but a poem on glory-bound
zealots and their zealotry.

Or poets. Poetry.

This is a poem about a late-late summer morning a long-long time
ago. Bright. This is a poem about an island. The only real island
in the world. Two simple upright structures. A ladder heavenward
with no rungs.

This is a poem about scope and heaven.

This is a poem about tall.

> ——*a parable: once a mad Frenchman strung a high-*
> *wire in an Impossible Place and he tiptoed out onto*
> *it. This is a story that can't be told too much. Or yes it*
> *can but I'm telling it again. I don't care that you're not*
> *listening. I can't hear you I can't hear you. He lay flat*

upon the wire a quarter-mile up. His name means small
in American. I can't hear you. You can barely hear him.
Fuck you death is what he is saying. Yes fuck you. Don't
look or look I couldn't care less.—

This is a poem about what was there

but now it's gone.

This is a poem about daring

to say good riddance.

Still Life with Heavy Layers of Paint

This is the story of his life he drew up around himself: the limnist tramps into the wheatfield.

As always he carries his instruments.

Or else a single instrument.

Some things to know: his brother has failed him. Which is to say the brother has procured himself a happy marriage and left his brother to it.

Which is not true or it is but it's a long story.

The brother-artist painted more than a sane man would paint. Layer on layer of paint applied toward an overgenerous beauty. Thick dabs or smears or else bullets of color. Relentless fields or skies or fields and skies of yellow.

An orderly system of hatching suggests an orderly system of mind

  ——*in the café I know that man who wears*
  the ponytail and his cargo shorts and I know him
  to be a sad man who sometimes knows himself
  to be sad and I know him to fetch the drinks
  with great dispatch and I believe that despite

or because of all this he will live a long life
and he will not be moved to cut a part of himself
off of himself even for the sake of some essential
or transcendent or timeless person place or thing. Which
is to say a woman and/or a painted picture. Amen.
Which is to say what I believe and what I know I take to
be the same thing. That is, even though I know this not
to be true.——

                       though orderly is not what it was at all.

900 paintings in nine years' time. At the end three per day.

Three good paintings per day will kill you dead.

There is nothing more true.

Which is not true.

What is more true is the thick untroubled yellow of the wheatfield.

What is more true is how a jot or series of jots or hatches or etches or even just plain brushstrokes makes the real sea-sway of a wheatfield somewhere in the south of France.

What is true is the single instrument he carries is what he uses to make a primary red deep hole in his very own hard chest.

Ink is a kind of stain of course. Blood on paper turns brown over time. Blood in that particular earth over time turns yellow and moves like a sea. Her skin is unblemished.

Sunkissed.

Her smile is the overgenerous white sun. His eventual fate:
separated from her beloved subject by a century and then some the
art historian fingers

——delicate instruments!——

the brown stains on an unsent letter
to his dear brother. His closest blood relation.

Is a perfect face as perfect as any kind of wheatfield real or
imagined or composed. Can beauty travel back in time to make
an ache—

——don't ask. We have to believe
you think you know.————

Still Life with White Noise

This is the story of his life he drew up around himself: what catches his interest will not hold his interest. That part is a given. One man's sneeze. Another man's bow tie.——*I just talked to Ellen I just talked to Ellen I said I just talked to that coffee place is where I am*——is what he hears the scruffy skin-and-bones espresso sipper say. All one tangled breath.

The lovely big-glasses girl he knows from somewhere twirls her tangled hair at the register.

Composition is a mess.

The songster says everything is collage. The poet who writes novels writes she said collage is the greatest of all the arts.

Which is not true. It is the opposite.

The other said what the other said.

~~Songster~~ Poet | ~~Poet~~ Songster.

Said is the same thing as wrote.

Given of course the poet writes novels. Etc.

——*this is going nowhere . . .*——

Etc.

——…in fits and starts…——

Ibid.

——I will abandon this. Put it down. Some dull metal tool I use to dig into the ground or else its opposite which is firmament which sounds the same but isn't. It's true. But it's a metaphor. I'll put down this digging tool. The foreman's red-faced spit-and-shout. I'll put it down and walk away.——

Rustic table. Whir. Milk froth tips our lap-top-man's long nose.

——I won't hold this heavy metal tool. Distort it with it the real ground or sky. I'll put it down. I promise you. It's true. 'Who are you talking to he said I said I just talked to Ellen hello…'——

All it takes is a sound bite.

If he could make it right for you he ~~would could~~ might.

Yes.

This is the story of his life.

It doesn't much matter what it means.

Still Life with Pinot Grigio

This is the story of his life he drew up around himself: here there is a pair of very young women in blue surgical scrubs who are almost too young for him.

But really they probably are too young for him.

In this café they serve the wine in juice glasses and it is not Paris and it is night but not quite night.

Which is to observe the dappled orange light and the stippling of leaves which are green or is green against the backdrop of the not-red brick wall across the street.

The women are too young or else not *not* too young and all of them are painfully beautiful.

———*A word is only what my body is or makes.*———

He stole that line almost from a painfully beautiful woman who is young but not at all too young but gone and that imaginary door has closed and he imposes his oblique and unrequited regrets upon you.

Also he imposes the words *painfully beautiful* upon you because they don't mean anything. Which is not true to the large majority of the world. They *do* mean something.

He will search for another way to say it all the same.

All of these women have their conspicuous asymmetries.

This eye spies the world from a different angle than the angle of that eye. A thick bandage nests in an elbow crook. A syntax knocks you in the jaw on purpose.

Etc.

There are two places to leave the place and two places to come into the place. Which sounds like four places but is in fact just two places because something is almost always something and something else all at once.

She waits tables and she dances.

She waits tables and she harbors a vocational hatred of the man who raised her. Or maybe what he did was abdicate.

Etc.

There are two old men and two old women at the big round table by the one door. Two bottles of wine. The one old man's wrist is casted. The other old man says nothing. The old women are still pretty and must have once been prettier still. One of the old men shovels braised lamb into the up-and-down machine of his narrow mouth. Pass the butter which someone does.

What conspicuous asymmetries these old people must have borne into this world.

The one who says nothing pays.

——ENDINGS——

Civilization: A History

This is the story of his life he drew up around himself: agriculture arose 10,000 years ago. Give or take.

The inside of a human belly is still an unfamiliar place for wheat and almost any other processed grain.

Ten thousand years of body makes a body makes a body and so on yields yes an evolutionary body of work.

Which is not true.

A body or better yet a series of bodies is a process a work if you're lucky in progress. Some things still it cannot process.

Which is to say the seeds of civilization.

10,000 years of foul shit.

The shark is a perfect thing. Eats. Swims. Fucks.

Not always but almost always in that order.

If a shark sleeps or shits it isn't what a human body knows as sleep or shit. Fucking goes without saying.

Plant the seed of human knowledge in a deep hole and make a garden of worthless weeds you never knew before.

The great fish moves beneath the black surface of a human mind and its high opinion of itself. It is and it is and then it isn't. The sea floor littered with this lineage of long-ago perfected bones.

Calculus

This is the story of his life he drew up around himself: preparations
to turn one square block into a street bazaar. Orange cones.
Folding tables. Port-a-potties. Police shoo the unfortunately
parked. A stream of men who glare purpose-fully and stalk the
block in some surely official capacity. They hiss into walkie-talkies.
Don one or more version of three different kinds of ID badge.
Conspicuously military is this linearity.

——lines intersect or else run parallel. Period.——

He sits on one end of the long table inside the café. Scribbling her
math homework in a spiral notebook at the other end of the long
table etc. sits a young woman.

*——all the young people walk or sit so erect. Such clear
elegant lines they make!——*

The math exists to prove the existence of parallel universes. Or at
the very least a world inside a world. It is said there is a statistically
significant distinction between the males of our species and the
females of our species. Namely: women see far more out of the
corners of their eyes. Once he took this as an invitation to believe
in infinite possibility. Even if she's not looking she is. And she is
and she is and so on. There's another way to see it now.

———she's not looking but she knows you are and hates you for it.———

This other potential trails off to the vanishing point. Which is to say it is infinite.

The vendors open their carts. The smudged sky threatens to open itself. Later there will be electrified music and plastic cups of pissy beer. In a tucked away corner of the alley one young man in a crisp white untucked shirt will vomit mostly foam. Some time ago one poet wrote of some bird or another circling out and out from its handler until it couldn't be seen or heard.

———I don't remember the rest. Something something stones. Something something sleep. Something something slouching. Then eventually Bethlehem.———

Down the table etc. she solves for *x* and *y* and graphs it out along the squiggly perpendicular axes she's drawn. He strains to see and not be seen. He fails on both fronts. She collects her things and without looking one way or another takes her infinite leave.

It was a double helix for what it's worth. Twisted strands.

What makes up all or any one of us.

The Names for Things

This is the story of his life he drew up around himself: he read figure as fugue

——*"a man thinks lilacs against white houses..."*
Etc.——

and confronted his sentence: a lifetime of misunderstandings exacerbated by the tricks and flourishes of a diminishing brain.

Any form of *draw* means so damn many things.

Drew for instance is a boy's name and a girl's too.

When he was a boy he said *crown* for *crayon*. He knew the difference but his tongue did not. Which is not true. It was his ears. A fugue is what he hears.

He draws a figure with a crown.

Once he was a young man sweating off a virulent bug in a dormitory somewhere. Painted cinderblock walls and shiny linoleum floors that could mirror a face. There and then he endured a days-long torture of deep but maddening sleep. Insatiable. All the while his brain a boil of fever dreams. He dreamed a whole language. Or

else what he dreamed was not the language itself but the desperate
devising of a language. Any language. Sentences syntax syllables: a
proverbial tabula rasa. All of it up to him. An unborn world.

——each time I started at the start a new start started.
What is the word for what for is for the for word for
for…——

He could not bear it and yet he kept on. In the manner of a child
poking a bruise. Picking a scab. No mother to tell him no.

The trouble with words is they mean things. To make a word first
you have to know the thing it means.

He once knew a boy named Drew no Gary who ate his own scabs.

Which is something his [Gary's] father taught him [Gary].

He knew a boy named Gibson who once put glue on his tongue
and was then frantic to get it off when no one laughed.

He couldn't think of the word for the way a mouth speaks when it
has no tongue in it or else when the tongue that's there is stuck and
can't move or else when the tongue that's there isn't really stuck
at all but a desperate little boy won't let himself use it because he
understands the word *glue* in that context to be an immutable
sentence.

He couldn't think of the word for *the boy in first grade who smells
funny and does stupid shit like putting glue on his tongue.* That is a
single thing that boy. *Gibson* is only one word for it.

Which is not true. Gibson is a name.

It is a last name and this particular Gibson used a last name for a first name. There is a word for that. A) *Paradox*. B) *Irony*. C) *Pretense*. Or else D) All of the above.

Explain your answer.

In college he read a book: *Certain Things Last*. That last word: does it mean *last* or *last*. The trick is it means both. Sherwood Anderson is two last names. Which is a clue. Which is not true. Or it is a half-truth and it sounds good

so close enough.

A fugue is a thing that gets away from you. A fugue is its own kind of boil. It swells and breaks like a fever.

Like a dream

impossible to know or figure.

Art in the Park

This is the story of his life he drew up around himself: he planted twenty-three miles of plasticized orange in the winding Central Park of his own mind or body or else the simple disembodied history of him. *It's just buzzing. It's just buzzing. You have to come here. It's the sound. Kids and people. You have to come here. It's the sound of it.* Someone in the crowd said all that.

It was the middle of winter for all this orange. The sleet and freezing rain. The squirrels. What do they think. And the fat dachshunds decked out in sweater vests. The creaking the aching groans the orange things I made made. The way they swayed. What is a lie. The art that you make in orange for everyone to see is a kind of lie.

Once when he was a boy there was a question regarding his veracity. It was a very important question.

He told a story about the bag lady of his mind who had been cast off. Discarded. She toted her bags in the park and no one noticed her until the city took its toll of her and once and for all she was sent back to from whence she came. Ashes to ashes.

But that's not what really happens to her. He cannot even recall all her potential ends:

Does she grow wings.

      ——*yes.*——

Is she an heiress. A prophet.

      ——*yes.*——

Midwestern beauty queen.

      ——*yes.*——

First female astrophysicist. Abstract Expressionist.

      ——*yes.*——

Minimalist.

      ——*yes.*——

Mother Mary. Marilyn Monroe. Etc.

      ——*yes and yes and yes.*——

And yes.

      ——*but remember this: the ducks don't leave. They stay
and swim through the winter slush. Propelled
by the furious invisible churn they make of their own
orange-webbed feet. Orange and orange everywhere
around them in my mind. None of this is holy. None
of this is holy. This is only art. Which is something
but is not wholly important. I am just one in the eight
millions. One in the eight millions. One man said
in the city of my mind that what I had done to his park
was as if I had squatted and shat in his yard. But he
forgets my mind and all this orange belongs
to me. Even the ducks. To me not him. Call to me dear.
All this orange. It sighs. I am only waiting. Amen.*

The Dream of Flight

This is the story of his life he drew up around himself: he was headed somewhere. Directly. In a machine. While all along the way other machines made a beautiful rubble of the cracked-slab manmade road.

Which is to say: they *re-did* the road.

While he was on it.

Which was necessary in a manner of speaking but not strictly necessary in the so-called Grander Scheme.

Indirectly necessary. Necessarily indirect. Something. Somewhere. Whatever. Etc.

Regardless. To pave the way over what was already smooth or smoothish needed to be made fully rough. This is called vision or revision, one.

A beaked machine bit rebar into smaller and smaller bits to build a very long row of nests. Unseen men in unseen moments had balanced chunks of gray rock like eggs or constellations in the crinkled irregular masses of wire. Nest after nest after nest in a rough corridor of nests.

Or else if not a corridor then at least a regular series of singular points on an otherwise infinite line.

Or not nests: galaxies. A galaxy of inanimate nests. Rough nest of inanimate galaxies. Startled smell of grasses seeps through the vent. Senses have senses.

Or not inanimate. *Intimate.*

>   *——o lord no. Trust me. Turn back. I know your aim:*
>   *you think you want to go there but you don't.——*

Nonetheless.

Machines have beaks and make ordered nests of broken metal bits and manmade rock. This all delights him in a way. It's all he recalls at the end of the day. Nests zooming back away. *Zoom* is a word and *crunch* is and *crinkle*. So is *bird*. And *fly*. And *fast*.

Once he was headed somewhere only where he doesn't remember. Instead he's only here now where he conjures up an erroneous sensation: warm living meat of a small wild bird in his palm. A real imagined bird. Imagined real. And *live*.

Long I.

>   *——I thought I told you...——*

Calm at first. But for the fluttery tick-tick-tock of the wild mechanics at her core. Then in a flurry of her sleek imaginary wings she bursts away. The energy of the universe.

Etc.

But then the energy of the universe is a constant. Which means it stays the same. Which means it stays just where it is. It doesn't ever go. It doesn't ever go *away*. Even though disorder grows——

———*yes yes Love. I know:*———

That's the only law we know.

——ACKNOWLEDGMENTS——

Portions of this work first appeared in *Posit, Black Warrior Review* (online), *Cavalier Literary Couture, 4ink7: An Unction from the Holy One*, and *DIAGRAM*. The quoted material in "The Names for Things" refers to Robert Hass's "Spring Drawing" and "Spring Drawing 2" in *Human Wishes*. There is also oblique reference to works, both extant and ephemeral, by the author himself and JD Salinger, Peter Benchley and Stephen Spielberg, Brigit Pegeen Kelly and Darcie Dennigan, and Christo and Jeanne-Claude, as well as various other works in the public domain.

TJ Beitelman is the author of six books—three poetry collections, a book of short fiction, a memoir, and a novel. He can be found on-line at tjbman.me or @tjbeitelman.